SHETLAND'S
WILD FLOWERS

A Photographic Guide

D. Malcolm

The Shetland Times Ltd.
Lerwick
1992

First published 1990
Second edition 1992
© Dr D. Malcolm

ISBN 0 900662 75 1

British Library Cataloguing-in-Publication Data

A catalogue record for this book is
available from the British Library

Printed and published by
The Shetland Times Ltd.
Prince Alfred Street, Lerwick, Shetland. ZE1 0EP

Contents

Preface to second edition

Following the publication of the first edition of this book, it soon became apparent that many readers would have welcomed the inclusion of Shetland names of the plants which are illustrated. I am therefore indebted to Laurence Graham of Tingwall who has kindly compiled such a list for this second edition.

It should be noted that even within Shetland a particular plant may be called by a variety of names depending on the locality in which it is found. Since it is not feasible to list all the local names of a given species, we have chosen to document that name by which it is most commonly known in the central Mainland area. Readers are referred to the Index of English names (pages 70 & 71). Where it is known, the Shetland name of a plant is inserted in italics following its corresponding English name.

Secondly, I wish to thank Richard Palmer of Oxford for pointing out an error in the first edition. The plant designated Marsh Speedwell (Plate 55) is in fact Blue Water-Speedwell which is also shown in Plate 87. Since it has not been possible to obtain a photograph of Marsh Speedwell for this second edition, it has been deleted and Plate 55 now illustrates Water Lobelia.

D. Malcolm, 1991.

". . . Consider the lilies of the field, how they grow; they toil not neither do they spin: And yet I say unto you, That even Solomon in all his glory was not arrayed like one of these."
Matthew 6 vrs. 28-29

Introduction

To both residents and visitors alike, the brief months of the Shetland summer present a very colourful spectacle. Barren pastures and dreary roadside verges seem overnight to be transformed into a welcome blaze of brilliant hues.

This guide-book is not an exhaustive record of all Shetland's flowering plants, but does include many of our more commonly occuring species with, in addition, a handful of unusual or otherwise special plants.

The most conspicuous feature of a plant to the layman is usually the colour of the flowers. With this in mind the plants in this guide have been grouped in sections based on the usual colour of their flowers.

It is important to note that the colour of the flowers of a particular species can vary. This most frequently involves subtle changes of shade but can at other times be quite dramatic, e.g., red campion (plate 27) can have white flowers, albeit rarely. Indeed, many plants whose flowers are normally blue or red may be found with white, pink or even lilac flowers. The reader's attention is drawn to this important point, both here and in the descriptive notes, as printing costs forbid showing these plants in all their variations.

Lists of habitats are presented and by consulting these the reader can see at a glance which plants included in the colour section are to be found in each habitat. It must be recognised that although helpful, divisions of habitats in this way are rather artificial as they tend to merge into each other and are seldom clearly defined.

Plants vary greatly in size according to the degree of shelter available. Although a very approximate indication of the size of each species is included in the notes, this should not be relied on too heavily, e.g., selfheal (plate 99) may be a mere 2 cm. high in exposed coastal grassland but over 20 cm. in more favourable situations away from the sea.

The user of this guide may occasionally find that his specimen does not exactly match the photograph of the plant he believes he has found. It may be an untypical example of the species illustrated; more likely, however, he is dealing with a closely-related plant not included in the illustrations. By consulting Scott and Palmer (1987), along with a comprehensive and fully illustrated book on British plants, he should accurately establish the name of his plant.

The descriptive notes have deliberately been kept simple and concentrate on the salient features only of the particular species shown in the accompanying photograph.

Acknowledgements

I wish to take this opportunity to thank those without whose assistance this guide-book could not have been made available.

First and foremost I wish to express my thanks and appreciation to Mr Walter Scott of Scalloway. I am indebted to him for his help in identifying many of the species shown in this book, for reading and correcting the entire script and for his many other useful suggestions.

I am grateful to the following friends for allowing me to use their photographs.

Mr R. J. Tulloch	Plates 15, 19, 20, 46, 51, 63, 75, 80, 84.
Dr M. Richardson	Plates 24, 31, 32, 36, 38, 41, 43, 64, 69, 85, 92, 98, 103, 104.
Mr A. D. D. Gear	Plates 39, 55, 78, 83, 86.
Mr R. G. Johnson	Plates 44, 96, 100.

Also, I wish to thank my wife, Priscilla, for typing the entire manuscript.

Finally, my thanks to all those who have been of assistance both by their encouragement and advice.

Glossary of Terms

Calyx — collective name for sepals whether separate or joined.

Corolla — collective name for petals.

Fellfield — areas of sparsely-vegetated gravel often supporting rare plants. Largest areas in Shetland occur on the serpentine of Unst and on the granite of Ronas Hill.

Flowerhead — a collection of tiny flowers arranged in a tightly packed head, as in dandelions, daisies, thistles and a few others.

Involucre — calyx-like structure immediately below a flowerhead, e.g. dandelions (plate 9).

Palmate — where the leaf is divided into leaflet lobes radiating from a common point, e.g. meadow crane's-bill (plate 96).

Palmate   **Pinnate**   **Pinnately lobed**

Pinnate — where the leaf is divided into leaflets borne symmetrically on either side of a common stalk. The division may be complete, e.g. tufted vetch (plate 95) or incomplete, e.g. autumn hawkbit (plate 7) when the leaf is then described as being pinnately lobed.

Rosette — a circle of leaves, usually at the base of the plant, and often lying flat on the ground.

Spur — a usually slender projection arising from the base of a petal or corolla.

Stipules — paired, leaf-like appendages arising from the base of the leaf-stalk.

Tendril — an outgrowth usually from the end of a leaf, often coiled or twisted, which enables a plant to grow upwards among surrounding vegetation by twisting itself around neighbouring plants, e.g. bush vetch (plate 47).

Trefoil — describes a leaf divided into three leaflets.

Umbel — a group of flowers with stalks all radiating out from a common point on the stem, e.g. hogweed (plate 70).

Abbreviations used in Notes

1. The abbreviations given below precede the English name and give the reader a rough indication of the size of the plant illustrated.

    (s) Small   Plants whose stems do not usually exceed 15 cm. (6") high, or in the case of trailing plants, do not spread more than 15 cm.

    (m) Medium   Plants between 15 and 38 cm (6" - 15"), in height or spread.

    (l) Large   Plants exceeding 38 cm. (15"), in height or spread.

2.   x indicates a hybrid species.

Plate 1 (m - l) **Marsh-marigold** *(Caltha palustris)*

Flowers yellow, up to 5 cm. diam., petals (actually coloured sepals) 5; stems smooth; leaves dark green, kidney-shaped, glossy. Native. Marshes, streams, ditches. Flowering late April-June.

Plate 2 (m - l) **Meadow Buttercup** *(Ranunculus acris)*

Flowers yellow, in forked terminal clusters, petals 5; sepals yellow, erect; stems branched, hairy; basal leaves deeply palmately lobed, long-stalked, upper leaves deeply segmented, stalkless. Native. Pastures, streamsides, roadsides, coastal banks. Flowering May-September.

Plate 3 (s) **Lesser Celandine** *(Ranunculus ficaria)*

Flowers yellow, 2-3 cm. diam., solitary, star-like, petals 8-12 opening only on bright days; stems spreading, succulent, hairless; leaves heart-shaped, long-stalked. Native. Streamsides, damp pastures. Flowering late March-June.

Plate 4 (s - m)
Lesser Spearwort
(Ranunculus flammula)

Flowers yellow, petals 5; sepals yellow; stems succulent, hairless; leaves elliptical to lanceolate, lower leaves stalked. Native. Streams, ditches, bogs, marshes. Flowering May-August.

3

Plate 5 (l) **Yellow Iris** *(Iris pseudacorus)*

Flowers yellow, showy; leaves stout, sword-like. Native. Streams, marshes, margins of lochs. Flowering July-early August.

Plate 6 (m) **Roseroot** *(Rhodiola rosea)*

Flowers greenish-yellow, in dense clusters; leaves thick, succulent. A native plant found chiefly on sea-cliff faces and ledges. Flowering May-July.

Plate 7 (s - m) **Autumn Hawkbit** *(Leontodon autumnalis)*

Flowerheads yellow, dandelion-like, 2.5 cm. diam., solitary; stems usually branched; leaves usually deeply pinnately lobed, terminal lobe long, narrow, pointed. Native. Pastures, meadows, etc.; found in a great many habitats. Shetland's most common dandelion-like plant. Flowering July-October.

Plate 8 (l)   **Perennial Sow-thistle** *(Sonchus arvensis)*

Flowerheads yellow, dandelion-like, 5 cm. diam., involucre with many yellowish hairs; stems branched, lower part hairless; lower leaves pinnately lobed with rounded lobes clasping stem; upper stem leaves shaped as spearhead with prickly margins. Introduced. Arable land, foreshores, beaches. Flowering July-September.

Plate 9 (s - m) **Dandelion** *(Taraxacum officinale)*

Flowerheads yellow, 3-5 cm. diam., involucres in many species turning outwards and downwards; flower stalk leafless; leaves in a basal rosette, of many shapes but basically shallowly to deeply pinnately lobed, the lobes normally pointing backwards. Several native and numerous introduced species grow in Shetland. Flowering May-June.

Plate 10 (s - m) **Common Bird's-foot-trefoil** *(Lotus corniculatus)*

Flowers yellow, often tinged red, in clusters, petals 5, the lower two fused to form the keel; stems straggling; leaves divided into 5 leaflets. Native. Dry grassy places. Flowering late May-August.

Plate 11   (m - l)
Meadow Vetchling
(Lathyrus pratensis)

Flowers yellow, in clustered spikes, petals 5, the lower two fused to form the keel; stems angled; leaves pinnate with a terminal tendril. Native. Rough grassy places, grassy sea-cliff ledges. Flowering late June-September.

Plate 12   (s - m)   **Kidney Vetch** *(Anthyllis vulneraria)*

Flowers yellowish-orange, clustered in a rounded flowerhead; base of flower surrounded by a woolly calyx; flowerhead encircled by a leafy involucre; stems bearing silky hairs; leaves pinnate. Native. Grassy sea-cliffs, sea-banks, pastures, roadside verges. Flowering late May-early July.

Plate 13   (m - l)   **Silverweed** *(Potentilla anserina)*

Flowers yellow, 2 cm. diam., petals 5; stems downy; leaves pinnate, leaflets toothed. A native plant of shingly and sandy beaches and coastal grassland easily recognised by its silvery leaves and red runners. Flowering late May-August.

Plate 14   (s - m)   **Tormentil** *(Potentilla erecta)*

Flowers yellow, 6-10 mm. diam., petals 4, notched; stems slender, straggly, finely hairy; leaves divided into three toothed leaflets, stipules conspicuously leaf-like. Native. Heathland, moorland, waysides, etc. Flowering May-September.

9

Plate 15　(s - m)
Slender St. John's-wort
(Hypericum pulchrum)

Flowers rich yellow, petals 5, reddish below with blackish dots on margins; stems hairless; leaves untoothed, tinged red. Native. Steep-sided streambanks, fellfield. Flowering late June-early September.

Plate 16　(s - m)
Lady's Bedstraw
(Galium verum)

Flowers yellow, tiny, in dense clusters, fragrant, petals 4; stems angled; leaves narrow, pointed, arranged in whorls. Native. Dry grassland, rocky stream-sides. Flowering July-August.

Plate 17   (m - l)   **Marsh Ragwort** *(Senecio aquaticus)*

Flowerheads yellow, daisy-like, large; leaves pinnately lobed, end lobe largest, blunt. Native. Pastures, streamsides, roadsides. Flowering late June-September.

11

Plate 18 (s - m) **Yellow Rattle** *(Rhinanthus minor)*

Flowers yellow, two-lipped with upper tinged indigo; stems smooth, square; leaves opposite, unstalked, toothed. Native. Grassland. Flowering late June-August.

Plate 19 (s - m) **Primrose** *(Primula vulgaris)*
Flowers pale yellow, on long, hairy stalks, petals 5, notched; leaves oval, wrinkled.
Native. Grassy cliffs, banks, pastures, roadsides, streamsides. Flowering chiefly
April-June.

Plate 20 (s) **Bog Asphodel** *(Narthecium ossifragum)*

Flowers yellowish-orange, star-like, in narrow spikes, anthers red, petals 6; stem erect; leaves narrow, clasping stem. A clove-scented native of wet heaths and moors. Flowering July-August.

Plate 21 (m - l)
Monkeyflower
(Mimulus guttatus)

Flowers yellow, two-lipped, the lower lip bearing red spots; stems succulent, hairless, flower-stalks hairy; leaves rounded, opposite, toothed. Introduced. Streamsides, ditches. Flowering July-September

Plate 22   (m - l)   **Mimulus x burnetii**

Flowers orange-yellow, two-lipped, calyx often petal-like, giving a double-flowered appearance; stems smooth; leaves rounded, opposite, toothed. Introduced. Ditches, streamsides. Flowering late June-August.

15

Plate 23   (m - l)
Fox and Cubs
(Pilosella aurantiaca)

Flowerheads reddish-orange, dandelion-like; stems long, slender, hairy and like the calyx, has the appearance of having been spattered with soot; leaves lanceolate, hairy, mostly from the base. Introduced. Waste ground. Flowering August-September.

Plate 24   (m)   **Marsh Cinquefoil** *(Potentilla palustris)*

Flowers reddish-maroon, star-shaped, petals 5, narrow, shorter than the sepals; leaves pinnate, leaflets oval, toothed. Native. Marshes, ditches, streamsides. Flowering late June-August.

late 25   (l)   **Marsh Thistle** *(Cirsium palustre)*
owerheads reddish-purple; leaves sharply spiny. Native. Rough marshy meadows,
)astal slopes, roadsides, etc. Flowering late June-August.

Plate 26   (m)   **Water Avens** *(Geum rivale)*

Flowers peach-red, cup-shaped, nodding, petals 5; sepals large, purple; stems down
lowest leaves pinnate, end lobe large, leaflets toothed, downy. Native. Wet plac
on rich ground. Flowering late May-August.

Plate 27   (m - l)   **Red Campion** *(Silene dioica)*

Flowers pinkish-magenta, petals 5, deeply cleft; sepal tube enlarged, 5-toothed, hairy; stems erect, hairy; leaves oval, pointed. Native. Grassy sea-cliffs, coastal banks, roadsides, old quarries. Flowering May-September.

Plate 28 (s - m) **Bell Heather** (*Erica cinerea*)

Flowers reddish-purple, globular, in clusters on woody branching stems; leaves whorls of 3 along the stem, dark green. Native. Dry heath and moorland, rock Flowering July-August.

Plate 29 (s - m) **Cross-leaved Heath** (*Erica tetralix*)

Flowers rose-pink, paler beneath, globular, clustered; stems slender, branching; leave narrow, pointed, greyish-green, in whorls of 4 along the stem. Native. Wet moorlan and heath. Flowering July-September.

Plate 30 (s - l) **Heather** *(Calluna vulgaris)*

Flowers pale purple, in spikes, petals 4; sepals pale purple, larger than petals; stems branching, woody; leaves small, opposite, feather-like. Native. Dry or wet moorland and heath. Flowering July-August.

Plate 31 (s) **Trailing Azalea** *(Loiseleuria procumbens)*

Flowers pink, small, petals 5; leaves numerous, oblong, opposite. Native. A very rare prostrate, evergreen undershrub found only on the Ronas Hill granite fellfield. Flowering late May-June.

Plate 32   (m - l)   **Herb-Robert** *(Geranium robertianum)*

Flowers pink, 15 mm. diam., in pairs, petals 5; calyx red, hairy; stems hairy; lea▪ deeply palmately lobed, fern-like, greenish-red. A probable native. Confined t◆ shingly beach at Boddam. Flowering late May-September.

Plate 33   (m)   **Red Clover** *(Trifolium pratense)*

Flowers pinkish-purple, in globular clusters; stems hairy; all leaves of the trefoil ty▪ the lower on long stalks, the two just below the flowerhead almost stalkless. Nati▪ Dry pastures, grassy sea-cliffs, roadside verges. Flowering late May-August.

ate 34   (m)
Ragged-Robin
(Lychnis flos-cuculi)

Flowers pink in forked clusters, petals each divided into 4 narrow lobes; calyx five-toothed, maroon, striped. Stems slender, slightly hairy; leaves lanceolate, paired. Native. Damp pastures, marshes. Flowering June-August.

Plate 35   (m)
Marsh Lousewort
(Pedicularis palustris)

Flowers pinkish-purple, two-lipped; stems much-branched; leaves pinnate. Native. Marshes. Flowering June-August.

Plate 36   (s)   **Lousewort** *(Pedicularis sylvatica)*

Flowers bright pink, two-lipped; stems numerous, unbranched. Native. Wet pastures damp heaths. Flowering late May-August.

Plate 37   (m)
Marsh Willowherb
(Epilobium palustre)

Flowers violet-pink, nodding when open, petals 4, notched; stems hairy leaves lanceolate, opposite. Native Streams,   ditches,   marshes Flowering July-September.

Plate 38 (s)   **Moss Campion** *(Silene acaulis)*

Flowers pink, almost stalkless on rounded moss-like cushions, petals 5, notched. Native. Rocky slopes near the sea, cliff-tops, fellfield. Flowering late April-June.

Plate 39 (s - m)   **Thrift** *(Armeria maritima)*

Flowers rose-pink, closely packed in a rounded flowerhead; involucre brown, papery; base of plant cushion-like, leaves very narrow. Native. Grassy coastal banks, cliff-tops, rocks, beaches, fellfield. Flowering late May-July.

Plate 40   (m)   **Pink Purslane** *(Montia sibirica)*

Flowers pink, petals 5, deeply notched; stems hairless; leaves rounded, fleshy, unstalked. Introduced. Garden outcast. Abundant at Kergord, in the roadside woodland near the house. Flowering late May-August.

Plate 41   (s)   **Wild Thyme** *(Thymus praecox)*

Flowers pinkish-purple, in clusters, two-lipped; parent stems woody, flowering stems four-angled, hairy on two opposite sides; leaves tiny, oval, opposite, fringed with hairs. An aromatic native of dry, grassy banks, pastures, stony heath, fellfield. Flowering June-September.

ate 42   (s)
rly Marsh-orchid
actylorhiza incarnata)

wers in spikes, usually flesh-pink but
en darker on sandy ground at the
uth end of Shetland; leaves unspotted,
oded at tip. Native. Rich marshy
stures, damp sandy dune pastures.
wering late May-early July.

Plate 43   (s)
Early-purple Orchid
(Orchis mascula)

Flowers purplish, with a long spur;
leaves oblong, mostly at the base of the
plant; stems with small sheathing
leaves. Native. Serpentine fellfield and
pasture. Very rarely in limestone
grassland elsewhere. Flowering late
May-early June.

27

Plate 44   (s - m)   **Northern Marsh-orchid** *(Dactylorhiza majalis subsp. purpurella)*

Flowers rich purple, in spikes; leaves spotted. Native. Marshes, damp pastures Flowering late May-July.

Plate 45   (l)
Spear Thistle
(Cirsium vulgare)

Flowerheads pinkish, large; stem cottony, sharply spiny; leaves deeply pinnately lobed, spiny. Native. Dry pastures, roadsides, upper parts of beaches. Flowering late July October.

ate 46 (s)   **Purple Saxifrage** *(Saxifraga oppositifolia)*

owers rosy-purple, petals 5; leaves small, opposite, unstalked. A rare shrub-like
ative of rocky coastal areas in the North Mainland of Shetland. Flowering late
arch-June.

late 47 (m)   **Bush Vetch** *(Vicia sepium)*

lowers purplish, in spikes of 2-6 blooms; stems weak, clambering; leaves pinnate,
nding in tendrils, leaflets oval, stipules two-lobed. Probably introduced. Grassy
oadside verges, arable land. Flowering June-August.

Plate 48   (m)   **Common Fumitory** *(Fumaria officinalis)*

Flowers pinkish, in spikes, tubular, tips tinged purple, spur rounded; stems wea
straggly, hairless; leaves pinnately lobed, fern-like, smoky-green. Introduced. In
near arable land. Flowering June-early October.

Plate 49 (l) **Creeping Thistle** *(Cirsium arvense)*

Flowerheads lilac, fragrant; stems spineless; leaves usually sharply spined. Probably introduced. Waste ground, roadsides, sandy soils. Flowering late June-September.

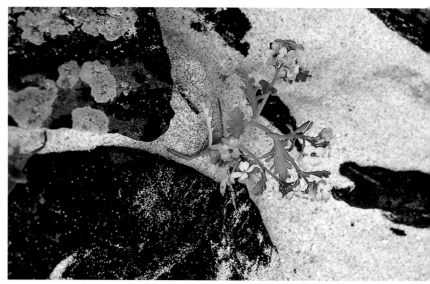

Plate 50 (m - l) **Sea Rocket** *(Cakile maritima)*

Flowers pinkish-lilac, sometimes white, fragrant, petals 4; stems succulent, branchir leaves pinnately lobed, fleshy. Native. Shingly and sandy beaches. Flowering Ju early October.

Plate 51 (m) **Cuckooflower** *(Cardamine pratensis)*

Flowers pinkish-lilac, sometimes white, petals 4; stems hairless; leaves pinnate, bas; leaves long-stalked, broader than the stem leaves. Native. Damp pastures, ditche Flowering May-August.

te 52   (m)   **Water Mint** *(Mentha aquatica)*

wers lilac, tiny, densely clustered in a rounded flowerhead, petals 4; stems erect,
ry; leaves opposite, short-stalked, toothed. An aromatic native. Streams, ditches,
hsides. Flowering August-October.

Plate 53 (s)
Heath Spotted-orchid
(Dactylorhiza maculata)

Flowers pinkish-lilac, sometimes white, in spikes; leaves lanceolate, often spotted. Native. Damp heathy pastures, moorland, serpentine. Flowering late May-July.

Plate 54 (s)
Heath Speedwell
(Veronica officinalis)

Flowers lilac, veined dark blue, in ere spikes, petals 4; stems hairy, creepir leaves oval, opposite, toothed, hai Native. Heathland, dry grassy plac Flowering June-August.

ate 55 (m)   **Water Lobelia** *(Lobelia dortmanna)*

ⱶwers pale whitish-lilac, drooping, two-lipped, held above the water on hollow,
ⱶfless stems; leaves in a submerged rosette. Native. Shallow water at the edge of
ⱶny lochs and pools. Flowering July-August.

Plate 56 (s) **Thyme-leaved Speedwell** *(Veronica serpyllifolia)*

Flowers bluish-lilac with darker veins, in spikes, petals 4; stems minutely hairy; leav
oval, opposite, unstalked, barely toothed. Native. Damp grassy places, roads
verges. Flowering May-July.

Plate 57 (s) **Eyebright** *(Euphrasia officinalis)*

A native genus with many closely-related species and hybrids. In general the flowe
are whitish-lilac, two-lipped, with a yellow spot and purple lines on the lower lip; ster
hairy; leaves deeply toothed. Eyebrights occur in many habitats from brackish coast
turf to upland heaths and fellfield. Flowering late May-July.

te 58   (s)   **Wood-sorrel** *(Oxalis acetosella)*
wers pale whitish-pink, solitary, petals 5; stems finely hairy; leaves trefoil, leaflets
rt-shaped. Native. Damp shady places, very rare. Flowering May-July.
otographed at Kergord where it grows as an introduction in the Lindsay Lee Wood.)

te 59   (s)   **Common Chickweed** *(Stellaria media)*
wers white, petals 5, cleft to base; sepals equal to or longer than the petals; stems
h a line of white hairs down one side; leaves oval, opposite, wavy, untoothed.
oduced. Arable land, waste ground, shingly beaches, sea-cliffs. Flowering April-
tember.

37

Plate 60   (m - l)   **Greater Stitchwort** *(Stellaria holostea)*

Flowers white, 15-18mm. diam., petals 5, deeply notched; stems slender, hairle
leaves lanceolate, opposite, pointed. An introduced species found only in some of t
Kergord woods. Flowering May-July.

Plate 61   (s - m)   **Bog Stitchwort** *(Stellaria alsine)*

Flowers white, star-like, petals 5, shorter than the sepals; stems square; leaves ov;
opposite, untoothed. Native. Ditches, streams. Flowering late May-August.

ate 62　(s)　　**Sea Sandwort** *(Honkenya peploides)*

owers greenish-white, petals 5; leaves paired, broad, fleshy, untoothed. Native.
ndy beaches. Flowering late May-July.

ate 63　(s)　　**Arctic Sandwort** *(Arenaria norvegica*
subsp. norvegica)

wers white, petals 5; leaves oval, opposite, fleshy. Native. A national rarity confined
the serpentine fellfield of Unst. Flowering late May-September.

Plate 64   (s)   **Shetland Mouse-ear** *(Cerastium nigrescens
                               subsp. nigrescens)*

Flowers white, large, petals 5, deeply cleft; leaves round, fleshy, purplish, ha
Native. Confined to the Unst serpentine fellfield and known nowhere else in the wo
Flowering late May-early August.

Plate 65   (s - m)
Common Mouse-ear
(Cerastium fontanum)

Flowers white, petals 5, notched;
sepals pointed, slightly shorter than
the petals; stems hairy; leaves
lanceolate, opposite, untoothed,
hairy. Native. Grows in many
habitats. Flowering late April-
September.

Goosegrass, Cleavers *(Galium aparine)*

lowers white, minute, petals 4; stems square; leaves lanceolate in whorls of 6-9. ative. A straggling plant covered in down-turned prickles. Shingly beaches. Flowering ily-September.

Sea Campion *(Silene vulgaris*
subsp. maritima)

wers white, petals 5, deeply cleft; sepal tube inflated; stems numerous, spreading; ves narrow, opposite, blue-green, hairless. Native. Shingly beaches, sea-cliffs, pentine fellfield. Flowering late May-August.

Plate 68   (m)   **Pignut, Earthnut** *(Conopodium majus)*

Flowers white, tiny, in umbels, petals 5; stems slender, arising from a small, brown
edible, underground tuber; leaves pinnate. Introduced. Pastures, roadsides. Flowerin
June-July.

Plate 69 (l) **Wild Angelica** *(Angelica sylvestris)*

Flowers whitish-pink, in large flowerheads up to 14cm. diam., composed of many smaller, rounded umbels; stems stout almost hairless; leaves pinnate, leaf-stalk expanded to form an inflated sheath. Native. Damp meadows, pastures, streamsides, etc. Flowering late July-September.

Plate 70   (l)   **Hogweed** *(Heracleum sphondylium)*

Flowers whitish-pink, in umbels, petals 5, notched; stems hairy; leaves pinnate, leaflet broad, hairy, lobed, leaf-stalk expanded into a large sheath. Probably introduced Rough grassy places, sandy pastures, churchyards. Flowering July-August.

Plate 71 (s)   **Daisy** *(Bellis perennis)*

Flowerheads solitary, composed of numerous tiny flowers, the central ones yellow, the outer white, conspicuous and often tinged crimson; stems hairy; leaves in a basal rosette, spoon-shaped, hairy. Native. Short grassland. Flowering March-October and during mild winters in favoured spots.

Plate 72   (m)   **Sneezewort**
(Achillea ptarmica)

Flowerheads creamy-white, daisy-like; stems finely hairy; leaves long, narrow, minutely saw-toothed. Native. Meadows, streamsides, loch margins, roadsides. Flowering late July-September.

Plate 73 (s - m) **Yarrow** *(Achillea millefolium)*

Flowerheads white, often pink, numerous, tiny, in flattened umbels; stems erec
downy; leaves pinnate, feathery. An aromatic native of dry pastures, roadsides, coast
grassland. Flowering July-September.

late 74   (m - l)   **Sea Mayweed** *(Matricaria maritima)*

lowers like large daisies, up to 5 cm. diam.; stems stout, usually prostrate; leaves
eshy, feathery. Native. Shingly beaches and sea-bird cliffs. Flowering late June-
eptember.

late 75   (s - m)   **Grass-of-Parnassus** *(Parnassia palustris)*

lowers white, 2 cm. diam., solitary, petals 5, veined; stems slender, clasped by a
ngle leaf; leaves in a basal rosette, stalked. Native. Damp pastures, marshes, stony
chsides. Flowering July-September.

Plate 76   (l)   **Meadowsweet** *(Filipendula ulmaria)*

Flowers in dense cream-coloured clusters; stems square, stiff; leaves pinnate, leaflets toothed, green above, silvery below. Native. A sweetly fragrant plant of streamsides, margins of lochs, damp pastures. Flowering late July-August.

ate 77   **White Water-lily** *(Nymphaea alba)*
 owers white, very large, opening fully on sunny days; leaves circular, large, floating.
 n unmistakable native plant confined to a few lochs in the West Mainland. Flowering
 ly-August.

ate 78   (m - l)   **Bogbean** *(Menyanthes trifoliata)*
 owers white inside, pink outside, in spikes, petals 5, fringed with white hairs on
 e inside; leaves divided into three large somewhat oval leaflets. Native. Deep peaty
 g-pools, lochs, streams. Flowering late May-early June.

49

Plate 79 (s - m) **White Clover** *(Trifolium repens)*

Flowers white, tiny, in globular flowerheads; stems creeping; leaves trefoil, often with a pale or dark band near the base of each leaflet. A sweetly fragrant native of pastures, grassy places, roadsides. Flowering late May-August.

Plate 80 (s)
Northern Rock-cress
(Cardaminopsis petraea)

Flowers white, petals 4; stems slender; lower leaves pinnately lobed, long-stalked. Native. Serpentine fell-field. Flowering May-August.

Plate 81 (s - m) **Common Scurvygrass** *(Cochlearia officinalis)*

Flowers white, sometimes lilac or mauve, in clusters, petals 4; leaves fleshy, heart-shaped, lower stalked, upper clasping stem. Native. Sea-cliffs, sandy or shingly beaches, coastal grassland, serpentine fellfield. Flowering late April-August.

Plate 82 (s) **Heath Bedstraw** *(Galium saxatile)*

Flowers white, tiny, petals 4; stems straggly; leaves pointed, arranged in whorls of 6-8. Native. Dry heaths, gravelly roadside verges. Flowering June-August. The common marsh-bedstraw *(Galium palustre)* is similar to the above but is larger with blunt-tipped leaves in whorls of 4-6. It grows in marshes and wet meadows.

Plate 83   (s)   **Fairy Flax** *(Linum catharticum)*

Flowers white, small, solitary, petals 5; leaves oblong, opposite, untoothed, distinct one-veined. Native. Heaths, dry grassland, sandy coastal turf, fellfield. Flowering la April-August.

Plate 84 (s - m) **Autumn Gentian** (*Gentianella amarella*)

lowers bell-shaped, whitish inside, reddish outside, petals 4 or 5, fringed inside with hite hairs; sepals 4 or 5; leaves opposite. Native. Sandy dune pastures, very rarely limestone grassland. Flowering late July-early September.

Plate 85 (s - m) **Field Gentian** *(Gentianella campestris)*

Flowers bluish-lilac, petals 4; sepals, 2 large overlapping 2 small; stems erect, smooth, branching; leaves opposite, unstalked, untoothed. Native. Chiefly dry stony pastures. Flowering late July-August.

Plate 86 (s - m)   **Sheep's-bit** *(Jasione montana)*

Flowers soft blue, occasionally white or lilac, tiny, in a globular flowerhead; involucre hairy; stems slightly hairy; basal leaves wavy, untoothed, hairy, upper leaves unstalked. Native. Dry grassland, grassy sea-cliffs, coastal banks, rocky streamsides. Flowering late June-August.

Plate 87 (m - l)   **Blue Water-speedwell** *(Veronica anagallis-aquatica)*

Flowers bluish-lilac, in opposite spikes, petals 4, stems succulent; leaves lanceolate, opposite, wavy, scarcely toothed. Native. Ditches and streams. Flowering July-September.

Plate 88　(s)
Spring Squill
(Scilla verna)

Flowers violet-blue, star-like, peta
6; stems smooth; leaves narrow, a
from the base of the plant. Nativ
Dry pastures, coastal grassland, se
banks, serpentine fellfield. Floweri
late May-June.

Plate 89　(s - m)　**Field Forget-me-not** *(Myosotis arvensis)*

Flowers blue, petals 5; leaves oblong, softly hairy. Introduced. Dry arable land, wasi
ground, sometimes on foreshores. Flowering late May-August.

Plate 90   (s - m)   **Creeping Forget-me-not** *(Myosotis secunda)*

Flowers characteristically sky-blue, sometimes bluish-white, 6-7 mm. diam., petals 5; stems hairy; leaves oval, alternate. Native. Streams, ditches, marshes. Flowering late June-August.

Plate 91   (s)
Changing Forget-me-not
(Myosotis discolor)

Flowers initially whitish or creamy, becoming blue, tiny (2 mm. diam.), in curving spikes; stems hairy; leaves lanceolate, alternate, hairy. Probably introduced. Dry grassland, arable ground. Flowering May-August.

Plate 92 (m) **Bugloss** *(Anchusa arvensis)*

Flowers blue, petals 5, joined; stems prickly; leaves lanceolate, wavy, prickly. Introduced. Sandy arable ground. Flowering June-October.

Plate 93 (m - l) **Oysterplant** *(Mertensia maritima)*

Flowers pink, becoming blue, bell-shaped, petals 5; stems sprawling, branching, succulent; leaves oval, bluish-green. A rare and decreasing native of a few shingly beaches. Flowering June-August.

Plate 94 (s - m)
Germander Speedwell
(Veronica chamaedrys)

Flowers bright blue with a white eye, in spikes, petals 4; stems weak with lines of hairs on opposing sides; leaves oval, opposite, toothed, hairy. An introduced species found chiefly on grassy roadside verges in the Tingwall Valley north of Scalloway. Flowering June-August.

Plate 95 (m)
Tufted Vetch
(Vicia cracca)

Flowers bluish-violet, in one-sides spikes of 12-36 flowers; stems hairy; leaves pinnate, leaflets narrow, pointed, stipules small. Native. Arable land, pastures, grassy sea-banks, sand-dunes, roadside verges. Flowering June-August.

Plate 96   (m - l)   **Meadow Crane's-bill** *(Geranium pratense)*

Flowers bluish-violet, large, petals 5; sepals hairy; leaves deeply palmately lobed. A garden escape found around or near dwellings. Flowering July-August.

Plate 97   (m)
Bluebell
(Hyacinthoides hispanica
*   x H. non-scripta)*

Flowers bluish-violet, sometimes white or pink, in spikes, bell-shaped; leaves long, narrow, all from the base of the plant. A popular garden plant often seen in grassy places near houses. Flowering late May-early June.

60

Plate 98   (s - m)   **Devil's-bit Scabious** *(Succisa pratensis)*

Flowers dark bluish-purple, tightly packed in a rounded flowerhead; involucre hairy; stems downy; leaves elliptical (the upper narrower), opposite, often blotched. Native. Pastures, marshes, streamsides, ditches. Flowering late July-early October.

Plate 99   (s - m)   **Selfheal** *(Prunella vulgaris)*

Flowers purplish-violet, two-lipped in a squarish spike; stems slightly hairy; leaves oval, opposite, scarcely toothed. Native. Grassland. Flowering July-August.

Plate 100   (s)   **Common Milkwort, Heath Milkwort**
(Polygala vulgaris, P. serpyllifolia)

Flowers usually dark blue or dark pink but often paler or nearly white, of an unusual shape owing to the two large wing-like coloured sepals; stems usually trailing; leaves small, narrow, alternate or opposite. Two very similar native plants of grassland, heaths, moors. Flowering late May-August.

Plate 101   (s)   **Common Butterwort** *(Pinguicula vulgaris)*

Flowers deep bluish-violet, solitary, two-lipped with white throat patch, spur pointed; leaves yellowish-green, forming a basal rosette. An insect-catching native species found on wet heaths and moors, dripping rocky streamsides. Flowering late May-July.

Plate 102 (s)   **Common Dog-violet** *(Viola riviniana)*

Flowers bluish-violet, solitary, petals 5, unequal, spur pale, curved, notched at tip; leaves heart-shaped, alternate, finely toothed, stipules usually fringed. Native. Dry pastures, rocky streamsides, grassy heathery sea-banks. Flowering late April-June.

Plate 103 (s)   **Alpine Lady's-mantle** *(Alchemilla alpina)*

Flowers pale green, tiny, in tight clusters; stems hairy; leaves palmately lobed, cut to base, green above, silvery below. Native. Granite fellfield on Ronas Hill. Flowering June-August.

Plate 104 (s) **Frog Orchid** *(Coeloglossum viride)*

Flowers greenish or brownish, in short spikes; stems angled; lowest leaves almost round, upper becoming narrower. Native. An inconspicuous orchid of dry, sandy, coastal pastures, cliff-top sward, limestone grassland and fellfield. Flowering late May-early August.

HABITAT LISTS

1. Meadows and pastures (including coastal grassland).

Angelica, Wild
Bedstraw, Lady's
Bird's-foot-trefoil, Common
Buttercup, Meadow
Campion, Moss
Clover, Red
Clover, White
Cuckooflower
Daisy
Dog-violet, Common
Eyebright
Fairy Flax
Forget-me-not, Changing
Grass-of-Parnassus
Hawkbit, Autumn
Hogweed
Milkwort, Common
Orchid, Early Marsh-
Orchid, Frog

Orchid, Heath Spotted-
Orchid, Northern Marsh-
Pignut
Primrose
Ragged-Robin
Ragwort, Marsh
Selfheal
Scabious, Devil's-bit
Sheep's-bit
Sneezewort
Speedwell, Thyme-leaved
Spring Squill
Thistle, Marsh
Thistle, Spear
Thyme, Wild
Vetch, Kidney
Vetch, Tufted
Yellow Rattle

2. Moorland

Bell Heather
Bog Asphodel
Butterwort, Common
Dog-violet, Common
Eyebright
Heath, Cross-leaved

Heather
Lousewort
Mouse-ear, Common
Orchid, Heath Spotted-
Tormentil

3. Damp streamsides, sides of ditches, margins of lochs

Angelica, Wild
Buttercup, Meadow
Celandine, Lesser
Cinquefoil, Marsh
Cuckooflower
Forget-me-not, Creeping
Grass-of-Parnassus
Iris, Yellow
Marigold, Marsh-
Marsh-bedstraw, Common
Meadowsweet
Mimulus x burnetii

Mint, Water
Monkeyflower
Primrose
Ragwort, Marsh
Scabious, Devil's-bit
Sneezewort
Spearwort, Lesser
Stitchwort, Bog
Water Avens
Water-speedwell, Blue
Willowherb, Marsh,

4. Lochs and streams

Bogbean
Lobelia, Water

Water-lily, White

5. Arable land

Bugloss
Chickweed, Common
Forget-me-not, Changing
Forget-me-not, Field
Fumitory, Common
Mouse-ear, Common

Ragwort, Marsh
Sow-thistle, Perennial
Speedwell, Thyme-leaved
Thistle, Creeping
Vetch, Bush
Vetch, Tufted

6. Woodland

Bluebell
Celandine, Lesser
Cuckooflower

Pink Purslane
Stitchwort, Greater
Wood-sorrel

7. Sea-cliffs, sea-banks, shingly and sandy beaches, foreshores

Angelica, Wild
Bedstraw, Lady's
Bird's-foot-trefoil, Common
Bugloss
Buttercup, Meadow
Campion, Moss
Campion, Red
Campion, Sea
Celandine, Lesser
Chickweed, Common
Dog-violet, Common
Eyebright
Forget-me-not, Field
Goosegrass
Herb-Robert
Mayweed, Sea
Milkwort
Orchid, Frog

Oysterplant
Primrose
Rocket, Sea
Roseroot
Sandwort, Sea
Scabious, Devil's-bit
Scurvygrass, Common
Sheep's-bit
Silverweed
Sow-thistle, Perennial
Spring Squill
St. John's-wort, Slender
Thrift
Thistle, Spear
Thyme, Wild
Vetch, Tufted
Vetchling, Meadow
Yarrow

8. Steep-sided streambanks (often rocky or ferny)

Angelica, Wild
Bedstraw, Heath
Bedstraw, Lady's
Bell Heather
Butterwort, Common
Celandine, Lesser

Cuckooflower
Primrose
Scabious, Devil's-bit
Sheep's-bit
St. John's-wort, Slender

9. Fellfield

Azalea, Trailing
Bird's-foot-trefoil, Common
Campion, Moss
Campion, Sea
Eyebright
Lady's-mantle, Alpine
Mouse-ear, Shetland
Orchid, Early-purple
Orchid, Frog
Orchid, Heath Spotted-

Rock-cress, Northern
Sandwort, Arctic
Scurvygrass, Common
Selfheal
Spring Squill
St. John's-wort, Slender
Thrift
Thyme, Wild
Vetch, Kidney

10. Roadside verges and banks

Bedstraw, Heath
Bedstraw, Lady's
Bird's-foot-trefoil, Common
Buttercup, Meadow
Campion, Red
Celandine, Lesser
Clover, Red
Clover, White
Crane's-bill, Meadow
Eyebright
Hawkbit, Autumn
Hogweed
Mouse-ear, Common
Orchid, Heath Spotted-
Pignut
Primrose
Ragwort, Marsh

Scabious, Devil's-bit
Selfheal
Sheep's-bit
Sneezewort
Speedwell, Germander
Speedwell, Thyme-leaved
Thistle, Creeping
Thistle, Marsh
Thistle, Spear
Thyme, Wild
Tormentil
Vetch, Bush
Vetch, Kidney
Vetch, Tufted
Vetchling, Meadow
Yarrow

11. Bogs and marshes

Bog Asphodel
Bogbean
Celandine, Lesser
Cinquefoil, Marsh
Cuckooflower
Dandelion
Eyebright
Forget-me-not, Creeping
Grass-of-Parnassus
Heath, Cross-leaved
Heather
Iris, Yellow
Lousewort, Marsh
Marigold, Marsh-
Marsh-bedstraw, Common
Mimulus x burnetii
Monkeyflower
Orchid, Early Marsh-
Orchid, Northern Marsh-
Ragged-Robin
Scabious, Devil's-bit
Spearwort, Lesser
Thistle, Marsh
Tormentil
Water Avens
Willowherb, Marsh

12. Heath and rough grassland

Bedstraw, Heath
Bell Heather
Daisy
Dog-violet, Common
Eyebright
Fairy Flax
Gentian, Field
Hawkbit, Autumn
Heath, Cross-leaved
Heather
Lousewort
Milkwort
Orchid, Heath Spotted-
Selfheal
Speedwell, Heath
St. John's-wort, Slender
Thyme, Wild
Tormentil
Yarrow
Yellow Rattle

References and Further Reading

1. The Wild Flowers of Britain and Northern Europe. By R. Fitter, A. Fitter and M. Blamey. (Collins.)

2. The Flowering Plants and Ferns of the Shetland Islands. By W. Scott and R. C. Palmer. (The Shetland Times Ltd.)

3. Wild Flowers. By H. L. Pursey. (Hamlyn.)

4. The Oxford Book of Wild Flowers. By B. E. Nicholson and S. Ary M. Gregory. (Peerage Books.)

5. The Pocket Guide to Wild Flowers. By D. McClintock and R. S. R. Fitter. (Collins.)

6. The Macmillan Field Guide to British Wildflowers. By F. Perring and M. Walters. (Macmillan Press.)

Index of English Names
with Shetland Names in brackets
(Plate Numbers)

Index of Scientific Names

robertianum, 32
Geum rivale, 26

Heracleum sphondylium, 70
Honkenya peploides, 62
Hyacinthoides hispanica x
   non-scripta, 97
Hypericum pulchrum, 15

Iris pseudacorus, 5

Jasione montana, 86

Lathyrus pratensis, 11
Leontodon autumnalis, 7
Linum catharticum, 83
Lobelia dortmanna, 55
Loiseleuria procumbens, 31
Lotus corniculatus, 10
Lychnis flos-cuculi, 34

Matricaria maritima, 74
Mentha aquatica, 52
Menyanthes trifoliata, 78
Mertensia maritima, 93
Mimulus x burnetii, 22
   guttatus, 21
Montia sibirica, 40
Myosotis arvensis, 89
   discolor, 91
   secunda, 90

Narthecium ossifragum, 20
Nymphaea alba, 77

Orchis mascula, 43
Oxalis acetosella, 58

Parnassia palustris, 75
Pedicularis palustris, 35
   sylvatica, 36
Pilosella aurantiaca, 23

Pinguicula vulgaris, 101
Polygala serpyllifolia,
   vulgaris, 101
Potentilla anserina, 13
   erecta, 14
   palustris, 24
Primula vulgaris, 19
Prunella vulgaris, 99

Ranunculus acris, 2
   ficaria, 3
   flammula, 4
Rhinanthus minor, 18
Rhodiola rosea, 6

Saxifraga oppositifolia, 46
Scilla verna, 88
Senecio aquaticus, 17
Silene acaulis, 38
   dioica, 27
   vulgaris subsp. maritima, 67
Sonchus arvensis, 8
Stellaria alsine, 61
   holostea, 60
   media, 59
Succisa pratensis, 98

Taraxacum officinale, 9
Thymus praecox, 41
Trifolium pratense, 33
   repens, 79

Veronica anagallis-aquatica, 87
   chamaedrys, 94
   officinalis, 54
   serpyllifolia, 56
Vicia cracca, 95
   sepium, 47
Viola riviniana, 102